PSALM 119

—

SCRIPTURE WRITING JOURNAL

THIS JOURNAL BELONGS TO

_____

_____

Introduction

—

Throughout Scripture, we are commanded and exhorted to meditate on God's Word (Psalm 1:2, 119:15, Joshua 1:8) and treasure it in our hearts (Psalm 119:11). We can accomplish this through daily Bible reading, Bible study, and Scripture memorization, but have you ever considered adding Scripture writing to your time in God's Word?

The discipline of writing Scripture can be a valuable addition to your regular Bible study time or a new way to meditate on His Word throughout the week. Writing out passages of God's Word forces us to slow down and focus more intently on the very words of Scripture. It can also be a new way to engage with God's Word as you take the time to read and write each verse, meditate on the meaning of the words, and treasure them in your heart. Writing also aids in memory. While reading, we may be tempted to rush through or quickly forget what we have just read, but slowing down to write the verses out on paper will help us remember the words of Scripture.

I have treasured your word in my heart so that I may not sin against you.
Psalm 119:11

On the following pages, you will find helpful tips and suggestions for Scripture writing, but the overall intention of this journal is to be a flexible and practical tool to help you develop your own system of writing Scripture.

—

It is our prayer that this journal will be a valuable addition to your time in God's Word.

Psalm 119

—

Psalm 119 is the longest psalm and the longest chapter in the Bible. It is comprised of twenty-two stanzas, each having eight verses—one stanza for each letter of the Hebrew alphabet. Psalm 119 is a wonderful passage to use for Scripture writing, whether you are just starting or have already made this practice a part of your Bible study time.

This beautiful and powerful psalm focuses on reverence and awe of God's Word, exhorting readers to meditate on it, spend time in it, and pray for it to influence their lives. In contrast to the praise of those who love the Word, the psalmist also expresses disdain for those who do not revere it. These contrasts provide an opportunity for reflection as you examine your heart and evaluate your own love for God's Word.

Nearly every verse of Psalm 119 makes mention of God's Word. Different terms used to identify His Word such as "law," "testimonies," "instruction," "judgments," "word," "precepts," and "statutes" are used to draw our attention to its beauty and glory that fill each page.

Many themes worth meditating on emerge throughout this psalm. As you read and write, look for the following themes, and make note of other themes you may identify:

- *Love for God's Word*
- *Following in the way of the Lord*
- *Repentance for not properly loving and reverencing the Word*
- *Grief over your sin*
- *Grief over man's sin*
- *Prayer for a right heart*
- *Praise of God's Word*

Scripture Writing

—

Beginning the practice of Scripture writing may seem like a daunting or intimidating task. Perhaps you struggle with simply sitting down to write a letter, are displeased with your own handwriting, or do not feel as though you have time to add another discipline to your busy schedule. But Scripture writing is just that—a discipline. Like any meaningful habit, it takes work and dedication to truly develop and reap its many benefits.

But take heart! Spending time in God's Word is always worthwhile. Following are some encouraging tips, suggestions, and additional practices for getting the most out of this time as you begin your Scripture writing journey.

HELPFUL TIPS & ENCOURAGEMENT

- *Do not rush or feel pressured to finish a day's passage in a certain amount of time. Take your time to meditate on the Word of God. If distractions or responsibilities arise, put down your pen, and return later to finish the passage.*

- *Before you begin writing, take time to learn the context of the passage. If you are writing a selection of verses from the middle of a chapter, go back and look at the surrounding verses. Learn about the author, audience, and purpose of the passage. Doing so will ensure that you are viewing and interpreting the passage correctly as you write and reflect.*

- *After you have written out a passage, take time to go back and study its message. Highlight and annotate key themes and concepts. Make note of what you need to apply to your own life.*

THINGS TO LOOK FOR WHILE WRITING

- *Commands*
- *Verses to pray*
- *Transition words*
- *Actions to take*

- *Personal application*
- *Character of God*
- *Traits of man*
- *Comparisons and contrasts*

TODAY IS **THURSDAY**   3 /25 /21

Write Psalm 119:17-24
"BOUNTIFULLY"
↑

Deal generously with your servant so that I might live; then I will keep your Word.

Open my eyes so that I may contemplate wondrous things from your instruction.

I am a resident alien on earth; do not hide your commands from me.

I am continually overcome with longing for your judgments.

You rebuke the arrogant, the ones under a curse, who wander from your commands.   > GOD CANNOT TOLERATE PRIDE!

Take insult and contempt away from me, for I have kept your decrees.

ALEPH

The first stanza of Psalm 119 proclaims blessings and happiness upon those who walk in the way of the Lord and keep His Word. The psalmist expresses his own desire to keep the statutes of the Lord and for the Lord to remain with him.

PRAYER

Ask the Lord to help you delight in Him and His Word. Thank Him for His Word and the joy and blessings brought by walking in His ways. Confess areas of your life in which you are not walking in step with Him today.

Write Psalm 119:1-8

BETH

*The second stanza of Psalm 119 begins with a
question. The psalmist asks how a person can keep
a pure life. This question is simply answered:
by keeping God's Word. The psalmist goes on to
declare his love for God's Word and commits to
following in its ways.*

PRAYER

*Ask the Lord to help you hide His Word in
your heart. Pray for remembrance of His precepts
when you are tempted and tried.*

Write Psalm 119:9 16

_____

_____

_____

_____

_____

_____

_____

_____

_____

_____

_____

_____

_____

_____

_____

_____

_____

_____

_____

_____

_____

GIMEL

In this stanza of Psalm 119, the psalmist requests that the Lord deal generously or bountifully with him. He laments those who would rather speak against him than follow the commands of God's Word. We are given a glimpse of God's character in verse 21—God cannot tolerate pride, and He desires that man will follow after Him.

PRAYER

Repent of times when your actions or decisions have been determined by pride rather than an adherence to God's Word. Ask the Lord for wisdom and understanding as you seek to delight in His statutes, regardless of man's opinion.

Write Psalm 119:17-24

ד

DALETH

This passage of Psalm 119 makes clear the contrast between our hopeless, fallen state and the life-giving power of God's Word. The psalmist acknowledges his despair and looks to the Word of God for life and revival. The psalmist desires closeness to God through His Word and is willing to take action to have that relationship (verses 30-32).

PRAYER

How do you see the contrast between our fallen humanity and the life found in a relationship with God through His Word? Ask the Lord to reveal areas of your life where you need to be strengthened by His Word. Ask Him to help you choose the way of truth, cling to His decrees, and pursue a life of obedience to His commands.

Write Psalm 119:25-32

_____

_____

_____

_____

_____

_____

_____

_____

_____

_____

_____

_____

_____

_____

_____

_____

_____

_____

_____

_____

_____

_____

_____

_____

HE

*In this stanza, we witness the psalmist's sincere desire
to understand the Scriptures. He asks the Lord to be his
teacher and instruct him in the way of His statutes.
He desires to not only understand the meaning of the
Word but also apply it to his life. In this stanza, we
see many different words used to describe the Word
of God (e.g., "statutes," "instruction," "commands,"
"decrees," "ways," "judgments," "precepts"). This
list reminds us that the Word of God is not merely
a collection of words and verses to memorize but the
very words, commands, and ways of God by which we
live — they direct our steps, give us understanding,
and instruct us in how we should live.*

PRAYER

*Ask the Lord to give you understanding of His Word.
Ask Him to speak to you through His Word and
reveal to your heart ways in which you are not living
in accordance with His statutes. Confess areas of your
life that you are keeping separate from His Word, and
strive to live according to His ways every day.*

Write Psalm 119:33-40

_____
_____
_____
_____
_____
_____
_____
_____
_____
_____
_____
_____
_____
_____
_____
_____
_____
_____
_____
_____
_____
_____
_____
_____
_____
_____

ו

WAW

*This sixth stanza of Psalm 119 addresses the freedom
and salvation found in knowing and loving God's Word.
The psalmist asks for wisdom and mercy in speaking
words of truth before those who taunt him. When we
study Scripture, we become stewards of its truth.
The psalmist finds freedom in this responsibility (verses
45-46). The freedom found in knowing and loving
God's Word is seen in contrast to the bondage found
in following the sinful ways of the world.*

PRAYER

*Ask the Lord for wisdom and understanding of His
Word so that you can steward it well and speak it to
those around you. Pray that you would correctly present
the Word of Truth (2 Timothy 2:15). Thank the Lord
for the freedom found in loving and following His Word.*

Write Psalm 119:11-48

_____
_____
_____
_____
_____
_____
_____
_____
_____
_____
_____
_____
_____
_____
_____
_____
_____
_____
_____
_____
_____
_____
_____
_____
_____

ז

ZAYIN

The psalmist writes of the comfort found in God's Word in verses 49–56. This stanza is filled with hope amidst the despair of the world. The psalmist finds comfort in the Word of God, even in the face of affliction and the derision of men. Furthermore, his remembrance of the Word comforts him.

|

PRAYER

Praise the Lord for the comfort that His Word provides. Ask Him to bring His Word to your memory when you are faced with trying situations.

Write Psalm 119:49-56

_____

_____

_____

_____

_____

_____

_____

_____

_____

_____

_____

_____

_____

_____

_____

_____

_____

_____

_____

_____

_____

_____

CHETH

In this eighth stanza of Psalm 119, the psalmist refers to the Lord as his portion. The Lord is his inheritance, substance, and all that he needs. The psalmist carefully examines how he has lived and the steps he needs to take, and he allows the Word of God to direct his steps and determine his actions. The psalmist closes this stanza by expressing his affection for others who fear and follow the Lord.

PRAYER

Is the Lord your portion? Do you find satisfaction in Him? Ask the Lord to fill any emptiness in your life with the truth of His Word. Pray that He would direct your steps. Thank Him for the fellowship you find with others who love Him, and pray for those relationships to flourish around His Word.

Write Psalm 119:57-64

_____

_____

_____

_____

_____

_____

_____

_____

_____

_____

_____

_____

_____

_____

_____

_____

_____

_____

_____

_____

_____

_____

_____

TETH

*"The Lord is good and upright" (Psalm 25:8),
and that truth is expressed in this ninth stanza. The
psalmist acknowledges that the Lord has dealt well
with him — not because his life has always been easy
but because he knows that the Lord is good and all
His works are good (verse 68). The psalmist makes
a shocking statement in verse 71. He says that his
afflictions have been good for him; they have taught
him the Lord's statutes. May we learn from his
perspective and remember that everything the Lord
allows to happen in our lives has a purpose.*

|

PRAYER

*Praise the Lord for His good, upright, and righteous
work in your life. Are there circumstances or tragedies
that you do not understand? Ask the Lord to give you a
proper perspective so that you can see Him in all things.*

Write Psalm 119:65-72

_____

_____

_____

_____

_____

_____

_____

_____

_____

_____

_____

_____

_____

_____

_____

_____

_____

_____

_____

_____

_____

_____

_____

_____

_____

י

YOD

The Lord created us, not to leave us alone but to lovingly guide us and shape us to be like Him. The psalmist knows this to be true and therefore sees the Lord's righteousness and fairness in judgment and affliction. Rather than turning away from God when trials and judgments come, he runs toward Him, knowing that all His ways are just.

PRAYER

When trials come, do you run to the Lord and His Word for comfort? When you have chosen sin over righteousness and are chastened by the Lord, what is your response? Repent of times when you have not chosen to run to Him. Praise Him for His righteous judgment and tender mercies.

Write Psalm 119:73-80

_____
_____
_____
_____
_____
_____
_____
_____
_____
_____
_____
_____
_____
_____
_____
_____
_____
_____
_____
_____
_____
_____
_____

KAPH

The eleventh stanza of Psalm 119 presents the psalmist in great despair. He is troubled both from within and without (verses 81 and 87), yet his hope is in the salvation of the Lord. He does not know when that salvation will come, but he has placed his trust in the promises found in the Word. Through all of his distress, he renews his determination to keep the Lord's precepts.

PRAYER

Are you going through a time of trial or testing? Do you feel, like the psalmist did, that your eyes are weary from straining to see when the Lord will rescue you from this trial? Pray that your faith will remain steadfast in the Lord during this season. Resolve to keep His precepts and to love His Word no matter the outcome.

Write Psalm 119:81-88

_____
_____
_____
_____
_____
_____
_____
_____
_____
_____
_____
_____
_____
_____
_____
_____
_____
_____
_____
_____
_____
_____
_____
_____
_____
_____
_____

ל

LAMED

*In this beautiful stanza, the psalmist praises the
Lord for three distinct attributes of His Word: its
endurance, life-giving power, and perfection (verses
89, 93, and 96). This stanza also draws our
attention to distinct attributes of God—that He
is unchanging, faithful, and perfect in all of His
ways. May we remember the truth found in the
first verse of the gospel of John, which says,
"In the beginning was the Word, and the Word
was with God, and the Word was God."*

|

PRAYER

*Praise God for His perfect Word. The inspired,
inerrant Word of God provides us with everything
we need. Through it, we are given new life. From
its pages, we learn who God is. From its precepts,
we are instructed in how we should live.*

Write Psalm 119:89-96

MEM

*There is no wisdom found apart from God.
This truth is made clear in this thirteenth stanza
of Psalm 119. The psalmist boldly declares that
the knowledge and wisdom he possesses exceed
that of his enemies, teachers, and elders — but only
because his wisdom is from God's Word. This stanza
reminds us that God's Word is the only source of
true wisdom and understanding.*

PRAYER

*When was the last time you told God that you loved
His Word? Examine your own heart to see where
His Word falls in your priorities. Do you run to it
for wisdom and understanding, or are you seeking the
world's wisdom first? Are its words sweeter than honey
in your mouth like the psalmist declares?*

Write Psalm 119:97 104

_____
_____
_____
_____
_____
_____
_____
_____
_____
_____
_____
_____
_____
_____
_____
_____
_____
_____
_____
_____
_____
_____
_____
_____
_____
_____
_____
_____
_____

נ

NUN

The opening verse of this stanza is doubtlessly one of the most familiar verses in Scripture, yet the truth of this verse becomes even more astounding when read in context with the rest of the passage. The psalmist proclaims that God's Word is illuminating his path and showing him the way in the midst of constant danger (verses 105 and 109–110). Despite this danger, his heart rejoices in the testimonies of the Lord.

PRAYER

Are you walking through a season of trial or confusion? In our fallen humanity, it is so easy to think, "I just don't know what to do" or "There's just no way out." But the Word of God is a lamp for our feet and a light for our path. Turn to the Word, ask the Lord to guide you, and trust that He will show you the way, one step at a time.

Write Psalm 119:105-112

SAMEK

This stanza of Psalm 119 covers three main aspects of the Word of God: its fullness, safety, and prevailing truth. The psalmist opens by contrasting his hatred for the empty, unstable thoughts of man with his love for God's law. The reader can conclude that God's Word stands in contrast to man's empty instability by being complete in its fullness. The Word is full and complete, providing safety and security (verses 114, 116, 117); it is full of prevailing truth in which we can confidently stand (verse 118).

PRAYER

Do you run to the Word for its safety and prevailing truth? We may not feel as though daily we are in physical danger, but we are in danger of falling prey to the world's philosophy. Pray and ask the Lord to renew your love for His Word. Commit to run to it daily for safety and security from the temptations of the world.

Write Psalm 119:113-120

AYIN

*In this stanza, we can sense the desperation of
the psalmist as he witnesses those around him
in violation of and disregard for the Word of
God. He proclaims his own love and reverence
for God's law and makes several requests. He
asks for protection from his oppressors and that
he would experience the faithful love of God,
gain wisdom and understanding from God's
Word, and the Lord would act in response to
those who violate His law.*

PRAYER

*When you see the world in violation of God's
Word, does it cause you to cry out to Him?
Are you desperate for those around you to
turn to Him? Ask the Lord for wisdom and
understanding of His Word as you seek to
follow Him in a world that does not.*

Write Psalm 119:121-128

PE

In the seventeenth stanza of Psalm 119, the psalmist sets forth a pattern for us to follow. He praises the wondrous, revealing nature of the Word, confesses his longing for the Word, and then proceeds to make several requests of the Lord based on His Word. The psalmist claims the promises made in Scripture and asks the Lord for grace, guidance, and deliverance from those who oppress him. He concludes the stanza with an expression of remorse over those who disregard the Word of God.

PRAYER

When we go to the Lord in prayer, we ought to begin in praise for His wondrous Word. Praise the Lord for all that His Word is. As you seek to follow Him, claim the promises found in His Word. Thank Him for His steadfast, unchanging love and care for His people.

Write Psalm 119:129-136

_____

_____

_____

_____

_____

_____

_____

_____

_____

_____

_____

_____

_____

_____

_____

_____

_____

_____

_____

_____

_____

_____

_____

_____

_____

TSADE

*In this stanza of Psalm 119, we find two underlying
themes nestled within the psalmist's song of praise.
The psalmist praises God for His Word's righteousness,
trustworthiness, purity, and truth. Yet, in the midst of
praise, the psalmist grieves once again over those who
despise the Word (verse 139). The other theme that
could easily be overlooked is found in verse 141. The
psalmist views himself in light of God's Word and
finds that he is "insignificant, and despised"
in comparison to its greatness.*

PRAYER

*It is good to praise the Lord for His Word and to dwell
on its beauty and truth, but how often do we pause to
grieve over those who do not know it? As we seek to
follow God's Word, are we maintaining a proper view
of ourselves? Pray and ask the Lord to give you a proper
view of self through the lens of His Word. Confess
any feelings of superiority over those who do not seek to
follow His Word. Ask the Lord to replace those feelings
with grief and give you a desire to see the lost come to a
saving knowledge of His Son through His Word.*

Write Psalm 119:137-144

_____
_____
_____
_____
_____
_____
_____
_____
_____
_____
_____
_____
_____
_____
_____
_____
_____
_____
_____
_____
_____
_____
_____
_____
_____
_____
_____
_____

QOPH

In this stanza, we see the psalmist's urgent and sincere desire for a devoted relationship with God through His Word. The psalmist realizes that this deep relationship he is seeking requires work and sacrifice. In verses 147 and 148, we see that he has given up sleep in order to pour over the Word of God. The life-giving, saving power of the Word is worth every ounce of devotion for the psalmist.

PRAYER

Have you given something up for a deeper relationship with God? Is devotion to His Word a priority in your life? Pray and ask the Lord to reveal anything in your heart that may be standing in the way of your relationship with Him. Commit today to prioritize time in His Word over earthly pleasures, empty activities, and wasted time.

Write Psalm 119:145-152

ר

RESH

In this beautiful stanza, the psalmist acknowledges three foundational truths about the Word that we would be wise to remember as well. First, he acknowledges that safety and salvation come from the Lord alone (verses 153-155). In the face of affliction, he keeps his eyes on the Lord above rather than on the dangers around him. Second, he proclaims the life-giving power of the Word (verses 154, 156, and 159). And lastly, he acknowledges the enduring truth found in God's Word (verse 160).

|

PRAYER

Praise the Lord for the safety, life, and truth of His Word. Confess areas of your life in which you are more focused on the worries around you than you are with the safety found in Him. Pray and ask the Lord to flood your heart with the wisdom and truth of His Word.

Write Psalm 119:153-160

SIN / SHIN

*In the second-to-last stanza of Psalm 119, the psalmist
opens with a reminder of the wonder, riches, and truth
of God's Word. He fears the Word, rejoices in its vast
treasure, and views it in stark contrast to the world's
falsehood (verses 161-163). May we run to the Word
for its wonder and riches! As verse 165 proclaims,
"Abundant peace belongs to those who love your
instruction; nothing makes them stumble." In the face
of every adversary, trial, and persecution mentioned in
Psalm 119, the psalmist ultimately finds peace
through the Word of God.*

PRAYER

*Do you view God's Word with awe and wonder? Do you
run to its eternal riches? Pray and ask God to renew your
wonder for His Word. Commit to the Lord that you will
keep His precepts and love His decrees. Ask Him to flood
your heart with peace from His Word today.*

Write Psalm 119:161-168

TAW

*In this final stanza of Psalm 119, we see the
psalmist once again reiterating his commitment
to the Word of God. He once again cries out for
understanding and asks the Lord to teach him His
statutes. In the final verse, he makes a comparison
that may seem shocking to us in retrospect of his
love for and commitment to the Word; he compares
himself to a lost sheep in need of being found.
May the cry of our hearts be that as we seek to live
our lives in step with the Word of God, we would
not lose sight of our Good Shepherd and Savior,
the seeker of our souls.*

PRAYER

*May the psalmist's closing prayer be the prayer
of our hearts today:*

*Lord, I love Your Word, and I will seek to follow
it. Teach me Your ways, and I will strive to live in
them. But Lord, I confess that my heart is prone to
wander. Like a lost sheep in need of the shepherd's
seeking, please seek your servant day by day and
guide me in Your truth.*

Write Psalm 119:169-176

*Thank you for choosing this
resource from The Daily Grace Co.*

CONNECT WITH US

@thedailygraceco
@kristinschmucker

CONTACT US

info@thedailygraceco.com

SHARE

#thedailygraceco
#lampandlight

VISIT US ONLINE

www.thedailygraceco.com

MORE DAILY GRACE

The Daily Grace App
Daily Grace Podcast